Contents

Our explosive Earth

Clouds of **ash** fill the sky. Red-hot liquid rock called **lava** runs down the mountainside. Rocks are falling from the sky. A volcano is **erupting**! Does this sound exciting? Get ready to be a volcano explorer!

Mount Etna, Italy

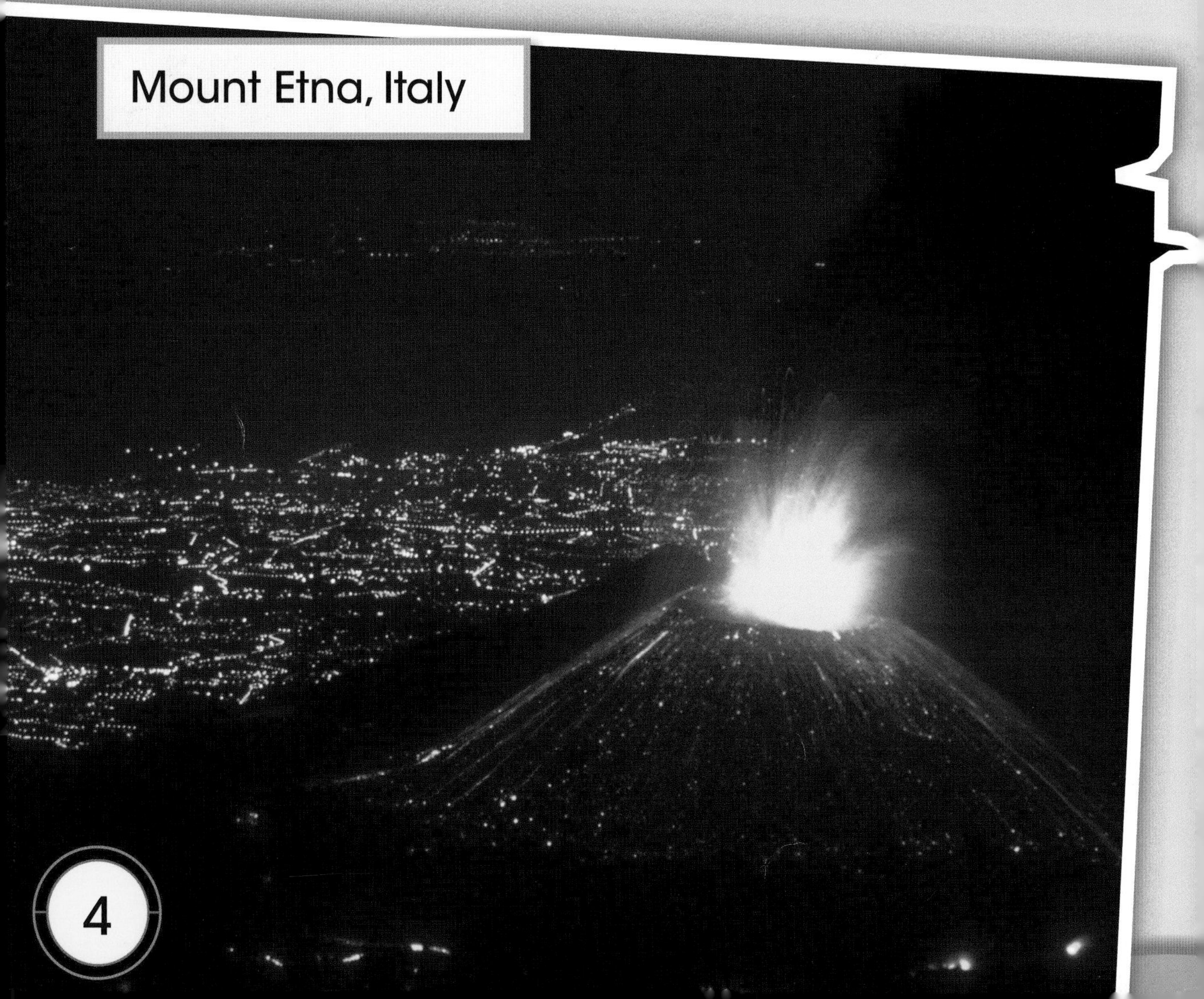

www.raintreepublishers.co.uk
Visit our website to find out more information about Raintree books.

To order:
Phone 0845 6044371
Fax +44 (0) 1865 312263
Email myorders@raintreepublishers.co.uk

Customers from outside the UK please telephone +44 1865 312262

Raintree is an imprint of Capstone Global Library Limited, a company incorporated in England and Wales having its registered office at 7 Pilgrim Street, London, EC4V 6LB – Registered company number: 6695582

First published in hardback in 2012
Paperback edition first published in 2013

Edited by Rebecca Rissman, Dan Nunn, and Sian Smith
Designed by Joanna Hinton Malivoire
Picture research by Elizabeth Alexander
Production by Victoria Fitzgerald
Originated by Capstone Global Library
Printed and bound in China by CTPS

ISBN 978 1 406 22570 9 (hardback)
15 14 13 12 11
10 9 8 7 6 5 4 3 2 1

ISBN 978 1 406 22577 8 (paperback)
16 15 14 13 12
10 9 8 7 6 5 4 3 2 1

British Library Cataloguing in Publication Data
Rosenberg, Pam.
Volcano explorers. -- (Landform adventures)
1. Volcanologists--Juvenile literature. 2. Volcanoes--Juvenile literature. 3. Volcanology--Juvenile literature.
I. Title II. Series
551.2'1-dc22

Acknowledgements
We would like to thank the following for permission to reproduce photographs: Alamy pp. 6 (© Lonely Planet Images), 15 (© Tony French), 21 (© M. Timothy O'Keefe); Corbis pp. 8 (© Sigit Pamungkas/Reuters), 11 middle (© Michael T. Sedam), 19 (© Roger Ressmeyer), 20 (© Roger Ressmeyer), 23 (© Francis R. Malasig/epa), 29 (© Randy Faris); Getty Images pp. 4 (Carsten Peter/National Geographic), 24 (Romeo Gacad/AFP), 26 (Roberto Campos/AFP), 28 (Philip and Karen Smith/Workbook Stock); Photolibrary pp. 11 bottom (Paul Thompson), 22 (Luis Castaneda), 25 (Photoalto); Science Photo Library pp. 7 (Dan Suzio), 9 (Jeremy Bishop), 11 top (David Parker), 12 (Gary Hincks), 13 (NOAA), 16 (Jeremy Bishop), 18 (ANAKAOPRESS/LOOK AT SCIENCES); Shutterstock pp. 5 (© beboy), 14 (© wdeon), 27 (© J. Helgason). Cover photograph of scientist examining lava at the Fournaise volcano, France reproduced with permission of Getty Images (Philippe Bourseiller/The Image Bank).

Every effort has been made to contact copyright holders of material reproduced in this book. Any omissions will be rectified in subsequent printings if notice is given to the publisher.

Some words are shown in bold, **like this**. You can find out what they mean by looking in the glossary.

Pam Rosenberg

lava

Liquid rock

A volcanic **vent** is a crack in the Earth's surface. Sometimes liquid rock, called **magma**, escapes from the vent. Sometimes it just dribbles out on to the Earth's surface. Other times it explodes into the air.

The liquid rock is called **lava** when it reaches the surface. Lava hardens as it cools. Over time, lava forms mountains.

This road is covered in hard lava.

Volcano scientists

People who study volcanoes are called **volcanologists**. They want to know more about why volcanoes **erupt**. They also want to find out when volcanoes will erupt. Then they can help to keep people safe.

Mount Bromo, Indonesia

This volcanologist is walking on **lava**.

Mount Etna, Italy

Fiery mountains

Not all volcanoes are the same. There are three main types of volcano.

- Cinder cone volcanoes are small. They have steep sides leading up to their **craters**.
- Shield volcanoes are large volcanoes. Their sides are not steep. They look like soldiers' shields lying on the ground.
- Stratovolcanoes are large, too. Their sides are steep near the crater, with gentle slopes at the bottom.

crater
cinder cone volcano

shield volcano

stratovolcano

Ring of Fire

Most volcanoes are found along the Ring of Fire. This is an area in the Pacific Ocean and along the coasts of the countries next to it. Some of the pieces that make up the Earth's **crust** come together in the Ring of Fire.

VOLCANO FACT

Robotic submarines help scientists study the underwater volcanoes in the Ring of Fire.

West Mata Volcano, Pacific Ocean

Active or dormant?

Some volcanoes are **active**. They often send out clouds of gas or **ash**. **Lava** flows down their slopes. Other volcanoes are **dormant**, or inactive.

Sakurajima Volcano, Japan

People living near dormant volcanoes feel safe. But there is no way of knowing for certain if a volcano will become active again!

Mount Vesuvius, Italy

VOLCANO FACT

Almost 2,000 years ago Mount Vesuvius **erupted** in Italy. It buried two large cities. Nobody knows when it will erupt again.

Volcanoes around the world

Volcanologists learn a lot by studying **active** volcanoes. They travel all over the world to find out more about them.

Mount Etna, Italy

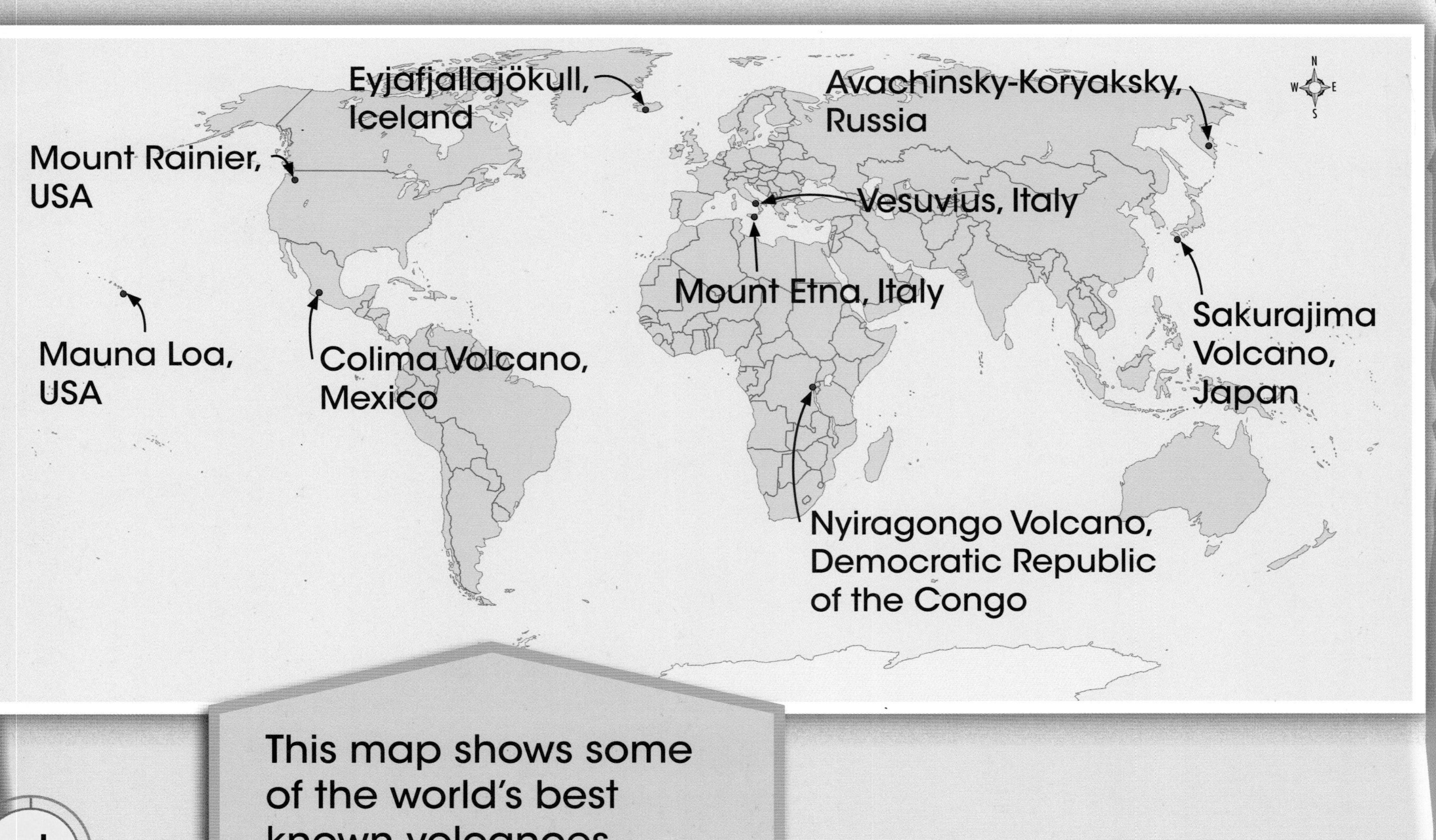

This map shows some of the world's best known volcanoes.

In the danger zone!

Some **volcanologists** walk on volcanoes, even when **lava** is flowing! They collect samples of **molten** lava. They need to wear fireproof gloves and clothing, and heavy boots.

fireproof glove

VOLCANO FACT

Molten lava samples are put in cans. Water is poured over the samples to make them go hard very quickly.

Sometimes **volcanologists** find out what kinds of gas are coming out of a volcano. These explorers need to wear gas masks when they work. Some gases can be deadly!

Scientists are watching the flow of this **lava** from a helicopter.

Volcano explorers don't always walk on volcanoes to collect information. Sometimes they use helicopters. They fly over the volcano to watch what is happening.

Gathering clues

No one is sure exactly when a volcano will **erupt**. But there are some clues that **volcanologists** look for.

Volcanologists look out for changes in the ground around a volcano.

Kilauea Volcano, USA

This scientist is using a computer to study earthquakes.

One clue is an increase in the number of earthquakes in the area. Another is an increase in some kinds of gases coming out of the volcano.

Keeping people safe

If **volcanologists** think an **eruption** might happen, they act fast. A team is sent to check the volcano. If they think an eruption is coming, they get people out of the area quickly.

Mayon Volcano, Philippines

Whole towns can be buried in lava and **ash**.

Red-hot **lava** and deadly gases can kill everything in their path.

The ash on this car in Argentina was carried by the wind. It came from the Chaitén Volcano in Chile.

Eruptions can cause problems for people many kilometres away from a volcano, too. Winds can carry **ash** for long distances.

In 2010 a volcano in Iceland **erupted**. Ash was blown over much of Europe. Airports were closed for days. This made it difficult for people to travel.

Eyjafjallajökull Volcano

VOLCANO FACT

The volcano in Iceland has a long name: Eyjafjallajökull! You say it like this: Ey-yah-fyah-lah-yoh-kull.

Becoming a Volcano explorer

Do you think the life of a volcano explorer is for you? Make sure you work hard at school. Study science and maths.

Be careful when you visit places with volcanoes!

Learn all you can about volcanoes. Visit places that have volcanoes. Keep track of your own volcano discoveries!

Glossary

active a volcano that is erupting or that has erupted recently

ash powder left behind after something burns

crater bowl-shaped hollow in the ground at the top of a volcano

crust hard outer layer of the Earth

dormant a volcano that has not erupted for a long time

erupt when rocks, ash, and lava are pushed out from inside the Earth with great force

eruption process of erupting

lava hot, liquid rock that comes out of a volcano when it erupts

magma layer of hot, liquid rock beneath the Earth's surface

molten melted, runny

vent opening in the Earth's crust from which magma and gases escape

volcanologist scientist who studies volcanoes

Find out more

Books

Our Angry Planet: Volcanoes, Anita Ganeri (Franklin Watts, 2009)

Volcanoes, Stephanie Turnbull (Usborne, 2007)

Volcanoes!, Anne Schreiber (National Geographic, 2008)

Websites

kids.nationalgeographic.com/kids/games/puzzlesquizzes/quizyournoodle-volcanoes/
Try this quiz to see how much you know about volcanoes.

www.esa.int/esaKIDSen/SEMMZKXJD1E_Earth_0.html
Visit this site to learn more about volcanoes and other natural disasters.

www.nhm.ac.uk/kids-only/earth-space/volcanoes/build-a-volcano/
Build a volcano and learn more about the different types of volcano.

Find out

Are there volcanos on other planets?

Index